I Can Do It!

I Can Ride My Bike

By Meg Gaertner

level
1
little blue
readers

www.littlebluehousebooks.com

Little Blue House is distributed by North Star Editions:
sales@northstareditions.com | 888-417-0195

Produced for Little Blue House by Red Line Editorial.

Photographs ©: Shutterstock Images, cover, 4, 6–7, 8–9, 11, 13, 14–15, 16–17, 19, 21, 23, 24 (top left), 24 (top right), 24 (bottom left), 24 (bottom right)

Library of Congress Control Number: 2022901331

ISBN
978-1-64619-578-7 (hardcover)
978-1-64619-605-0 (paperback)
978-1-64619-658-6 (ebook pdf)
978-1-64619-632-6 (hosted ebook)

Printed in the United States of America
Mankato, MN
082022

About the Author

Meg Gaertner enjoys reading, writing, dancing, and being outside. She lives in Minnesota.

Table of Contents

I Can Ride My Bike **5**

Glossary **24**

Index **24**

park

I Can Ride My Bike

I ride in the park.

I ride in the forest.

forest

I ride in the driveway.

driveway

I ride in the parking lot.

parking lot

I ride in the street.

street

I ride on the sidewalk.

I ride on the beach.

beach

I ride on the path.

path

I ride with my helmet.

I ride with my family.

family

Glossary

beach

forest

family

helmet

Index

D
driveway, 8

H
helmet, 20

P
park, 5

S
sidewalk, 14